Academic Presenting and Presentations

Teacher's Book

Further components in this series

Student's Book   ISBN 978-1-911369-24-0

Downloadable videos   www.linguabooks.com/app

Video DVD   info@linguabooks.com

www.linguabooks.com

Academic Presenting and Presentations

A preparation course for university students

Teacher's Book

PETER LEVRAI

AVERIL BOLSTER

Academic Presenting and Presentations
A preparation course for university students

Teacher's Book

Peter Levrai and Averil Bolster have asserted their right under the Copyright, Designs and Patents Act, 1988 to be identified as the authors of this work.

ISBN: 978-1-911369-25-7

Second edition

Editor: Ann Claypole

Proofreader: Marie-Christin Strobel

Copyright © 2016, 2019 LinguaBooks

LinguaBooks
Elsie Whiteley Innovation Centre
Hopwood Lane
Halifax HX1 5ER

www.linguabooks.com

Contents

"I hope I remember everything," said Toni.
"You won't," said Trapp. *"That's how you learn."*

Louis Sachar, The Cardturner

Foreword

Academic Presenting and Presentations is a training course designed to help students cultivate academic presentation skills and deal with the various presentation tasks they may be required to fulfil during the course of their university studies. The material in the Student's Book is suitable for a global audience and can be used in a wide range of contexts in the field of EAP (English for Academic Purposes), since it helps develop presentation skills and also deals with broader topics of interest in a study-oriented context such as research and plagiarism. The material emphasises higher level task-achievement rather than discrete language points since experience shows that this is the area that most students find especially difficult.

A key tenet of the course is that effective presentation skills alone will not lead to a successful academic presentation. As well as technical presentation skills, students will also have to appreciate the key features of academic presentations (such as soundness of argument and use of referenced support) and also be aware of the expectations of different genres of academic presentation, from seminar presentations introducing a paper to more sophisticated research presentations. Each unit of *Academic Presenting and Presentations*, therefore, focuses on a different presentation genre, building students' awareness of not only how to present effectively, but of how to present appropriately in an academic environment.

As it is a presentation course, the accompanying videos form an integral component of this course. The videos consist of two types of presentation: **Learning Presentations**, which give advice to students and **Sample Presentations**, which illustrate different types of presentation.

The presentations are available online and can be found on the *Academic Presenting and Presentations* website at:

http://www.linguabooks.com/app

A boxed set of Video DVDs is also available from the publishers. This contains videos of all the Sample Presentations and Learning Presentations in a format suitable for playing on a standard DVD player.

This Teacher's Book includes general guidance for class work, detailed notes on each unit and details of the theoretical rationale on which the course is based.

Concept and Structure

Basic principles

Presenting is an important part of university life. Students in different disciplines may well be expected to present as part of their studies. These may be developmental presentation tasks, such as presenting a paper to introduce a seminar discussion, or more formal, assessed presentations, which are the culmination of coursework assignments.

The aim of this course is to give students advice about different types of presentation task and also show them examples of presentations that they can analyse to identify successful presentation techniques. Throughout the course, students will also have ample opportunity to prepare and deliver the kinds of presentation they may be asked to give as part of their studies.

The core assumption of this course is that technical presentation skills alone will not enable students to deliver successful *academic* presentations. The definition below highlights what academic presentations mean in the context of this course.

- **Definition:** An oral academic presentation is a clear articulation of ideas, based on and referencing sources or research evidence, in which the presenter leads the audience to logical and sound conclusions. Effective presentation skills are needed so the audience can follow the presentation easily, but an academic presentation must have substance. Through the presentation the presenter must analyse and evaluate information, making their reaction and position clear to the audience.

Information in an academic presentation must be verifiable and the presenter must have a wider and deeper knowledge of the topic than that presented in the body of the presentation. A presentation should lead to discussion and further debate, with the presenter able to respond to audience questions competently. Different genres of academic presentation (e.g. presenting a paper, research presentations or problem-solution presentations) will require students to employ an appropriate structure.

A presentation-driven course

Academic Presenting and Presentations is built around presentations. This is based on the belief that the more presentations students see, the more clearly they will develop their ideas about what makes a presentation successful and what constitutes an appropriate academic presentation. There are two types of presentation in *Academic Presenting and Presentations:* **Learning Presentations** and **Sample Presentations**.

- **The Learning Presentations (LP)** give students information and advice about different aspects of presenting. While the focus of these presentations is on the advice given to students, they can also be used as examples of presentations in themselves and analysed for issues such as useful presenting language or delivery techniques.

- **The Sample Presentations (SP)** give students a chance to see different types of presentation in action and therefore become familiar with different genres of academic presentation. The emphasis while watching these presentations is on seeing how different presentations work structurally and how a presentation can be delivered successfully. A review of these presentations is provided in each unit of the Student's Book and useful language is highlighted there. If you are not familiar with the variety of genres of academic presentation, it is strongly advised that you study these reviews in advance of teaching the course.

For both Learning Presentations and Sample Presentations, a main task is given in the Student's Book and there are further worksheets at the end of the Student's Book which can be used at your discretion. One of the aims of the course is flexibility and it is expected that the material will be exploited by the class tutor to meet the students' needs. As the class tutor, you should also consider yourself a key learning aid in terms of modelling presentation techniques.

Methodology

Academic Presenting and Presentations is designed to expose students to a variety of different presentations and give them the opportunity to develop and deliver a range of presentations themselves. The methodology of the course is based on three main techniques.

- **Observe-Hypothesise-Experiment:** Throughout the course students will be expected to watch a presentation and consider issues such as organisation, language and delivery. In this way they can build up a profile of what they think works in a presentation and use this to develop their own presentation style.

- **Content-based instruction:** The Learning Presentations not only provide information and advice about presenting, but also serve as examples of presentations to be learned from. The topics in the Sample Presentations are chosen as relevant to students from different disciplines and, as well as being examples of presentations, engage students in thinking about other academic skills such as teamwork and researching.

- **Genre analysis:** In the same way that students may be expected to incorporate certain step during different types of essay, they should be using similar steps in different types of presentation. This means *Academic Presenting and Presentations* goes deeper into the structure of a presentation than simply introduction-body-conclusion. Students are encouraged to structure their presentations according to the objective of their presentation and their audience.

Class management

A presentation classroom should be lively. Encourage students to see the preparation process of a presentation as an active process. Rather than silent scripting or rehearsal, encourage students to prepare and practice as if giving the presentation. In this way, they can think about what they want to say, how they want to deliver it and what gestures to use.

For this reason, the Student's Book does not give any specific guidance on class management, e.g. whether to work in pairs or in groups. This is because the organisation of your group will depend on the logistics. The aim should be to give each student as many opportunities present as possible, either to small groups or to the whole class. Teachers should also be aware of the distracting impact of simultaneous presentations taking place in different parts of the room.

Since rehearsal is a vital step in the presentation process, consider using a carousel system along the lines of speed dating. Have some students sitting around the room whilst other students move from one person or group to the next, delivering a part of their presentation and then moving on. This type of practice could be particularly beneficial for more reticent students, providing them with multiple opportunities to practice the delivery of their presentation in a relatively stress-free way. There should also be opportunities for students to present to the full class, since managing a larger audience is a skill presenters need to develop.

Timing

Students are expected to spend a third of the course time following the material in the Student's Book, a third of the time preparing presentations and a third of the time giving presentations and receiving feedback on them. There is an average of two hours input material per unit (videos, language exercises, class discussion etc.) and students may also have to do a considerable amount of work outside class time, researching information for their presentations. However, ample class time should be given to presentation preparation and practice.

Aims

The overall aim of the course is to help students prepare for a range of academic presentation genres and develop an awareness of the features and characteristics of an academic presentation. The objective is to help students not only to present well, but to do so in an academically appropriate way.

The main aims and objectives for each unit are outlined in the notes to each unit in this Teacher's Book. At the start of each unit in the Student's Book, there is a Unit Aims box which asks students to consider specific questions which focus their attention on the main teaching points of the unit. Aims are presented in this way in order to encourage students to think about the upcoming unit and provide a focus for later reflection.

These opening questions could be dealt with either in small groups or used for general class discussions. They could also provide the opportunity for additional presentation practice, with a student presenting their (group's) answers one or more of the questions.

At the end of the unit, these questions could be returned to for a further class discussion in order to check how much of the course the students have taken on board and to see how their ideas have developed. This will help mark the progress of the course and indicate where more work may be needed.

Presentation tasks

There are eleven formal presentation tasks in *Academic Presenting and Presentations*, although you may also take other opportunities (e.g. summary of a group discussion) to give students presentation practice. The earlier presentation tasks are designed to help students become comfortable presenting generally. From Presentation Task 7 onwards, the academic integrity of the presentations take on a greater significance. There must be reliable and academically suitable material in the presentations and, consequently, they will take longer to prepare. The page numbers in the following table refer to the Student's Book.

Presentation Task		Page	Objective
1	Presentations and me	23	to give students the opportunity to present on a familiar topic and to enable the tutor to see where students are starting from
2	Presenting a paper	48	to see how students are able to deliver a presentation on a text (or texts) they have read
3	Presenting a team	59	to give students the opportunity to develop a presentation in a team context and reflect on the group presentation process
4	Presenting a poster (poster provided)	64	to enable students to see how different groups deal with presenting the same information
5	Presenting a poster	66	to give students the chance to design their first visual aids
6	The persuasive presentation	72	to give students the opportunity to develop and deliver a persuasive presentation without the need for academic support
7	The academic persuasive presentation	74	to see how effectively students are able to develop an academically sound and supported persuasive presentation
8	Progress presentation review	85	to give the students the chance to present their ongoing smartphone project to the group and gain feedback on the direction of their project
9	Problem/solution presentation on scripted presentations	94	to see how students synthesise input texts into an academic presentation discussing how to present without a script
10	Presenting data	103	to see how students are able to select data selectively and purposefully to support their presentation
11	Smartphone presentation	106	the final capstone presentation of the course designed to bring together all the learning of the course

Preparing presentations

When students are preparing their presentations, monitor the class carefully and provide any assistance students might need with particular vocabulary items or ways of expressing their ideas. This is an opportunity to focus on things like individual learner pronunciation issues. When students are preparing, push them towards having flexibility of expression. Ask them how else they could say the same thing. Encouraging a variety of expression will help students rely less on fully scripted presentations and enable them to present more naturally. Varied repetition of different sections of a presentation can be very useful in terms of developing a more natural presentation style.

Preparation can also be set as homework, but make sure there is some class time for preparation to enable you or peers to give feedback before the delivery stage. To try to help students really develop their presentation skills avoid giving too little preparation time. A poorly prepared or poorly rehearsed presentation has limited learning opportunities besides learning to prepare more thoroughly. Even a one-minute presentation is going to take time to develop, so factor this into the planning.

When students are working together in the preparation stage, push them to notice positive and poor presentation features and ask what aspects of another person's presentation style they could use to improve their own presentation skills.

During this stage, also consider how students are using scripts/notes. A general contention of *Academic Presenting and Presentations* is that full scripting should be avoided. Early in a presentation course, however, students might want the security of a script. Encourage them towards the use of note cards and bullet points. A note-card template is provided as one of the photocopiable worksheets at the back of the Student's Book. If students are using notecards, ensure they are using them for bullet points and main ideas only. During rehearsals, monitor students to make sure that as they become more familiar with their presentation they rely on their script or notes less and less.

Presentation practice

Whenever students are presenting, make sure you encourage them to **present** rather than simply talk. During the course, they should learn to stand, move and talk in a distinct presentation style which is different from their conversational voice. Always encourage students to present confidently, from the moment when they greet the audience to when their presentation closes. You might, for example, get a student to repeat the opening of a presentation a number of times until it comes smoothly and naturally.

There are various worksheets provided at the back of the Student's Book which can also be used to guide peer feedback. Once you have got some way into the course and the students have a clearer idea about presenting and the features of an academic presentation, you should also consider using class-generated presentation feedback sheets. Having students develop their own presentation evaluation sheets will help crystallise their thinking about what makes a successful presentation.

It is also important that presentations fit the requirements of the task. A two-minute presentation should take two minutes. Your students will have to learn what is and is not possible within a particular timeframe and adjust the content of their presentation accordingly. Don't be concerned about stopping students if they have gone significantly over the time limit you set. They have to learn to appreciate what can be covered in a presentation in a fixed amount of time.

Presentation questions

The question and answer part of a presentation is highly valued by lecturers as it is this part of the presentation where a true measurement of a student's understanding can be taken. It is also expected that a successful academic presentation will initiate wider discussion. Although strategies for dealing with questions are not covered until Unit 6, students should be asking questions after presentations throughout the course and should be encouraged to identify when someone deals with questions well or fails to do so.

Presentation feedback

Although this is a presentation skills course, it is an *academic* presentation skills course. This means presentations have to be considered on a deeper level than technical presentation expertise alone. Content matters. When giving feedback, ensure students consider issues like strength of argument, overall success of presentation in meeting its aim, use of support and evidence. As well as tutor feedback, peer feedback should also be strongly encouraged.

It can be very valuable to see presentation style as a member of the audience through the use of video. Once students have become more comfortable presenting, you could consider videoing their presentations. This could be potentially stressful, so only do it with student consent and, initially, avoid whole group feedback or showing the video to the whole group. The student could watch their presentation and provide their own feedback to you regarding its strengths and areas which could be improved. Video can also be very motivating if students are able to see how their presentation skills develop, either through repeated practice of the same presentation or over the full *Academic Presenting and Presentations* course.

You can also provide opportunities for students to redeliver their presentations, based on the initial feedback.

Overview

Unit	Topic	Presentation skill	Language skill	Academic skill
1 Introduction to Presentations	Presentation Skills	Basic presentation structure	Signposting language	
2 What Is an Academic Presentation?	Academic Presentations	Identifying good presentation techniques	Noticing useful language Pronunciation skills – developing a presentation voice	Recognising what makes a presentation academic
3 Seminar Presentations 1: Presenting a Paper	What is Research?	Referring to the work of others	Using the language of stance	Summarising a short paper Synthesising papers
	Project Introduction	Approaching A Topic		
4 Elevator Pitch Poster Presentations	Teamwork	Developing clear visual aids	Diplomatic language	Teamwork and group presentations
5 Persuasive Presentations	Research Methodologies	Changing the mind of the audience	Persuasive language	Evaluating your argument
6 Seminar Presentations 2: Presenting Progress	Smartphone Project Presentation	Using presentation software	Talking about the past and future	Giving a project progress report Dealing with questions
	Project Review	Giving A Progress Presentation		
7 Problem/ Solution Presentations	Plagiarism	Presenting without a script	Paraphrasing	Avoiding plagiarism Referencing
8 Presenting Research	Research Presentations	Presenting data	Describing tables and graphs	Finding sources
	Project Presentation	Giving A Final Presentation		

Learning Presentations

Unit	Presentation Title
1	**1.1 – Introduction To Presentations** – The Basics
	1.2 – What Makes A Good Presentation – Making Sure Your Presentation Has A POINT
	1.3 – Presentation Task – Presentations and Me
2	**2.1 – The Academic Presentation** – Key Features of Academic Presentations
	2.2 – Presentation As Performance – Developing Your Presentation Voice
3	**3.1 – Presenting A Paper** – Make Your Opinion Known
	3.2 – Presenting More Than One Paper – Horizontal vs. Vertical
4	**4.1 – Group Presentations** – Everyone Has A Role
	4.2 – Designing A Poster – Making An Impact
	4.3 – Elevator Pitch Presentations – Making A Point in 30 Seconds or Less
5	**5.1 – Being Persuasive In An Academic Presentation** – Substance Over Style
6	**6.1 – Presenting Progress** – Two Approaches
	6.2 – Using Presentation Software – Helping the Audience Follow Your Message
7	**7.1 – Problem/Solution Presentations** – Cause and Effect
8	**8.1 – Presenting Data** – Statistics, Tables and Graphs
	8.2 – Research Presentations – Finding and Filling A Gap

Sample Presentations

Unit	Presentation Title
2	**2A – Electric Vehicles** – The way to a brighter future?
	2B – An Evaluation of Barriers to Electric Car Use
	2C – The Ion Plus – Finus Sales Report and Projections
3	**3A – Introduction to Research** – 3 Types of Research
	3B – Research Methodology: An Introduction – The Objectives And Motivations of Research
	3C – What is Research?
4	**4A – Managing Teamwork** – Roles and Responsibilities
5	**5A – Electric Vehicles** – The way to a brighter future (*Presentation 2A*)
	5B – Choosing a Research Method – Striking A Balance
6	**6A – Are Smartphones Destroying Language?**
7	**7A – Avoiding Plagiarism** – Citing and Note-making
8	**8A – Undergraduate Research Methods** – Using Online and Library Sources

In the Student's Book, **Learning Presentations** are introduced like this:

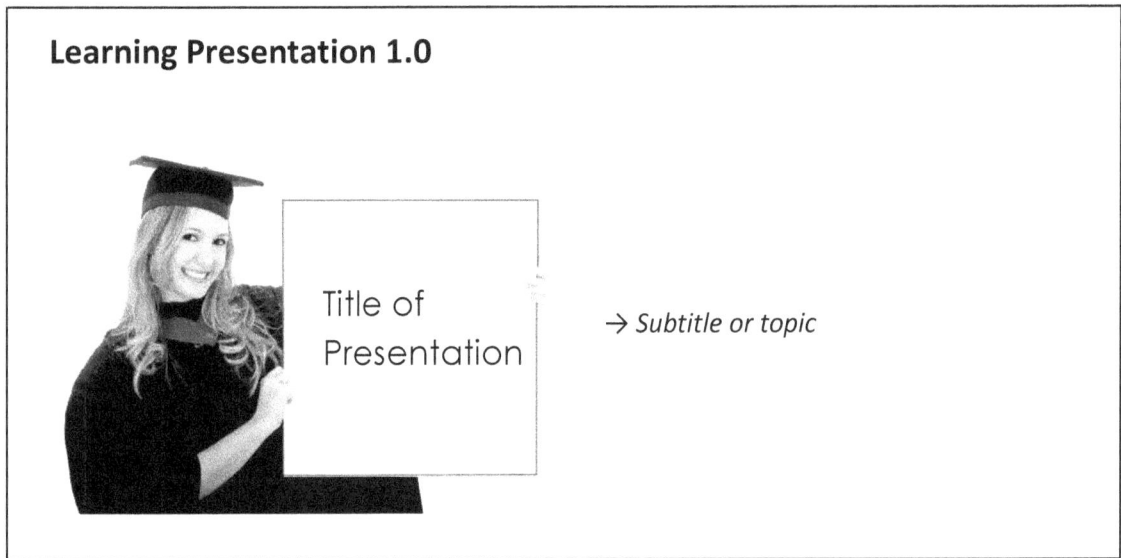

Learning Presentation 1.0

Title of Presentation → *Subtitle or topic*

And **Sample Presentations** are identified like this:

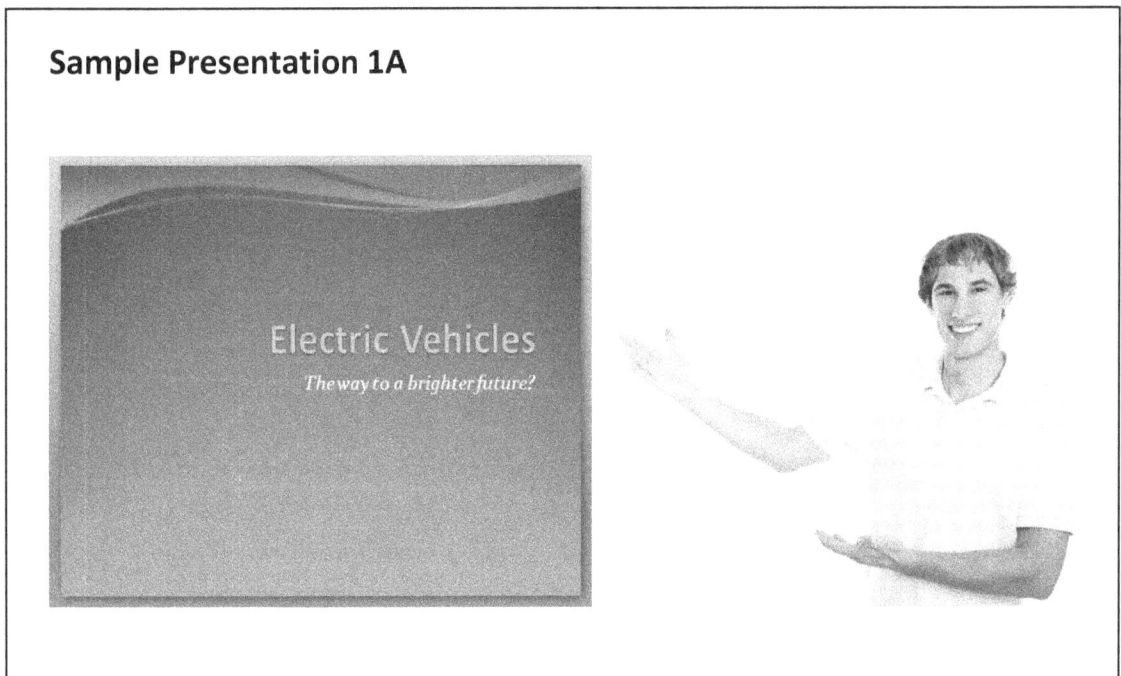

Sample Presentation 1A

Electric Vehicles
The way to a brighter future?

Unit 1
Introduction to Presentations

This unit is designed to give students a basic overview of presentation skills. At this stage the academic factor is ignored.

Aims & Objectives
To raise students' awareness of generic presentation skills
- provide students with an overview of presentation structure
- provide students with a tool to help develop good presentations

---

The lead-in aims discussion for this unit should be given some time so you can identify how much experience your students have of watching or delivering presentations. It will also be useful here to emphasise the various reasons why people present, to reinforce the idea that the students are starting to learn a skill which will be very important to them in future life.

This will also be an opportunity for expectation setting in the sense of telling students that during the course they will be presenting a lot as the only way to improve presentation skills is through practice.

LP 1.1 – Introduction to Presentations
This is a long video which provides information about

- types of presentation
- considering the audience
- dealing with nerves
- basic structure & Signposting language
- how to use *Academic Presenting and Presentations*

Due to the length, this video could be broken into sections and discussion could take place between sections (e.g. why is the audience important, how can nerves be controlled etc.). You could have the students review the whole video for homework. However, it is also good for students to see an extended presentation, as they may have to give lengthy presentations themselves.

Signposting language

Signposting language is important in presentations. You might want to replay certain sections of the video so students can recognise how the presenter moves between sections. Suggest students have a presentation vocabulary book where they can make notes of useful expressions.

However, it is important to remind students that they are not game show hosts. Since the content of an academic presentation is what matters and time may be limited, such language needs to be kept to a minimum. For example, at the start of Presentation 1.1 there is quite a lengthy overview of the structure of the presentation. While this may be appropriate for a longer presentation, it would be a waste of valuable time in a short (10 minute) presentation.

A good presentation

At this point, the students are not thinking about academic presentations but presentations in general. Brainstorming ideas in small groups or whole class should generate ideas for dos and don'ts of presenting. Encourage students to make notes which they may return to and edit as they watch the upcoming Learning Presentation.

Before watching the Learning Presentation you might ask a couple of students to give a very short (1 minute) presentation about what they or their group thinks makes a good presentation. Getting students to present without visual aids is an important step in developing their presentation skills so they will come to see visual aids as a support for a presentation which, while very useful, may not always be necessary.

LP 1.2 – What Makes A Good Presentation?

This presentation emphasises things students need to consider when planning a presentation: **A**udience, **P**urpose, **O**rganisation, **I**mpact, **N**otable, **T**heatre. There is a photocopiable worksheet in the back of the Student's Book which students can use when planning a presentation to consider each of these. It could also be used when watching Sample Presentations so the students can consider how well the presenter has planned and delivered their presentation and, most importantly, if the presentation has fulfilled its purpose with the audience.

Presentation Task 1

This is the first main Presentation Task of the course. After watching the Presentation Task (**Learning Presentation 1.3**) spend some time as a whole group thinking of different ways of focusing this topic to encourage students to see how they can approach a topic and consider ways of making it interesting for their audience.

The purpose of this presentation is to give everyone a chance of presenting to a group. Presentation feedback should focus on positive aspects of the presentation, be they organisation, delivery or idea related.

Set a time-limit for the presentation suitable for the logistics of your group (2-3 mins recommended) and make sure there is time for questions at the end of the presentation. Perhaps tell the students they have to think of at least one question they could ask connected to the presentation they have watched. Feedback should also cover how well, or not, the students dealt with the questions.

Unit 2
What is an Academic Presentation?

This unit considers the particular features which make a presentation academic. Essentially this means highlighting the issue of *intertextuality* with students and emphasising that an academic presentation fits into a wider debate and has to be supported by sources.

> **Aims & Objectives**
> To raise students' awareness of key features of academic presentations
> - provide an overview of the defining features of academic presentations
> - focus students on the technical aspects of presenting (use of body language and voice)

The initial discussion on the features and types of academic presentation may not take long, depending on how much students are aware of already. To help inform their discussion you could show the three Sample Presentations before asking them to try to come up with ideas of the defining characteristics of an academic presentation.

> **SP 2A, 2B & 2C**
> A brief analysis of the Sample Presentations is provided at the back of the Student's Book. Before looking at the analysis, watch each presentation and encourage students to discuss whether it was
>
> a) a good presentation
> b) an academic presentation.

You could also have them watch the presentations with the A POINT worksheet from Unit 1 to reinforce the habit of looking at a presentation from that perspective and to give the students the opportunity to hypothesise about the audience and purpose of each presentation. This is also useful because when you have identified the academic presentation, you can point out that a weakness in the A POINT approach is that it ignores the need for **Support** in an academic presentation.

Once students have identified 1B as the academic presentation, discuss the features that made it clear it was an academic presentation (e.g. use of referencing and citation, development of an argument).

Looking at these samples is a way to emphasise that a good presentation does not necessarily make for a successful academic presentation.

You could also exploit these videos for delivery issues. Later in this unit, students are going to consider use of voice. Video 2A is particularly useful for highlighting the use of stress and pausing. You can also draw attention to instances when the presenter pauses because they are not sure what to say next.

LP 2.1 – The Academic Presentation
Now that students have developed a better idea about the features of an academic presentation, you can show this Learning Presentation to re-emphasise the elements that make a presentation academic. This could lead to a discussion of how Sample Videos 2A and 2C could be made more academic. While presentation 2C might be quite hard to change into a presentation suitable for the academic sphere, presentation 2A could be changed quite easily. The emotive side of the presentation would have to be dropped and the reasons and arguments the presenter makes would have to be supported by evidence.

LP 2.2 – Presentation As Performance
From the outset it is important to encourage students to develop a presentation voice. Typically, presenters speak differently when presenting than when talking. Before watching the Learning Presentation, ask students to brainstorm what leads to effective delivery when presenting. Make notes of their ideas on the whiteboard and after watching the video, add to their ideas based on their revised suggestions.

This task requires them to practice delivering a script and the emphasis should be on delivering this as naturally as possible. Emphasise that they don't have to be word perfect so there is no need to stop if they say the wrong thing. The focus is on how they say it. Encourage them towards larger stresses and hesitations than they might otherwise use. Also model different ways of saying the same thing, showing how the meaning and focus can change based simply on the use of voice.

Once they have become confident delivering the text, encourage them to do so without looking at their books. This puts the emphasis back on the message rather than delivery. Make it clear you do not expect them to remember the text perfectly, but you do want them to present the main ideas of the text, and present them while using strategies to vary their voice to increase the impact of the presentation on the audience. This will be an important step to lead students away from relying on a script.

Unit 3
Presenting a Paper

A common presentation task which cuts across all academic fields is the presentation of a paper or papers the student has read. This is done as both a measure of understanding of the text and also to initiate a class discussion.

Aims & Objectives
To raise students' awareness of the expectations of presenting a paper in a seminar
- emphasise the need for analysis and evaluation in presenting a paper
- introduce students to the language of stance
- encourage students to synthesise if they have to present more than one paper

---

Since the focus of this unit is presenting a paper, it is important that the students have short papers to base their presentations on. This means the start of this unit requires students to read Text 1 and Text 2. This could be set for homework or perhaps in class time, some of the students reading Text 1 and the others reading Text 2 and then discuss their papers in pairs. After this, students could read the other text and determine how successfully it was explained by their partner. An advantage of this method would be highlighting from the outset how different readers take different things from the same text.

Depending on the needs of your students, you might use this opportunity to introduce some reading strategies you feel they may find beneficial. In terms of note-making it would be useful at this point to draw the students' attention to the difference between summary notes (notes which provide a summary of a text) and responsive notes (notes which contain students' reactions to what they have read e.g. highlighting points they feel are most useful, writing questions about things they don't understand or want to know more about).

Since this is a presentation course there is no need to go into great depth about reading strategies or varieties of note-making, but it is important that students understand that they need to have a reaction to what they read. If that reaction is that the paper is difficult to read and not particularly useful, then that is fine. Within a seminar presentation they could talk about those issues.

SP 3A & 3B
Prior to watching these presentations, you could ask students to present the paper they have read to the group, particularly if you have divided the reading between students. However, it is important that students are familiar with *both* papers before watching these presentations.

SP 3A – this is a relatively poor presentation of a paper. While the presenter identifies the main points of the paper, there is no interpretation, reaction or evaluation. After watching this presentation, ask the students if they think it was a good presentation. Then ask if they learned anything new from the presentation they didn't learn from the paper.

SP 3B – This is a more successful presentation in that the presenter is selective with the information presented and, more importantly, has a clear reaction to the ideas in the paper and suggests what those ideas mean in their own context. Focus students' attention on the way the presentation is not a repetition of the paper's perspective, but is rather a clear expression of the presenter's perspective.

LP 3.1 – Presenting A Paper
Prior to watching this presentation, have the students brainstorm what makes a successful paper presentation, based on the sample video presentations they have watched and any presentations of the papers you may have asked the students to develop. While watching LP 3.1, have students add to these ideas if anything new comes up.

Language Focus – when discussing papers, students are going to have to make their reactions clear. This introduction to the language of stance will provide students with some different ways of expressing their opinion about a paper. With higher level students, there could be an opportunity for brainstorming alternative ways of showing a positive or negative reaction. With lower level students the main focus should be on showing that different ways of expressing opinion are possible and that in an academic presentation the presenter's (supported) opinion should be clear.

LP 3.2 – Presenting More Than One Paper
Students may also be asked to present more than one paper, or more than one input e.g. students could be asked to present an academic paper and a journalistic article on the same topic. The approach to this task suggested in *Academic Presenting and Presentations* is to find common features across the papers and give a presentation which speaks about the papers simultaneously rather than presenting the first paper then the second with no connection between the two.

SP 3C – The sample provided does this reasonably well in terms of making a connection between reasons for research and types of research from the two different papers. The presenter's own understanding is also clear.

Presentation Task 2

Depending on the strength of your students this could be done in different ways. You could ask them to present one of the papers, Text 1, Text 2, Text 3 or Text 4 or make it more challenging by asking them to present two or more of the papers. This presentation task can be done individually, in pairs or in small groups.

As an alternative to the research papers in the book, you could also source papers from within your students' field of study. In a single discipline class this might be a good approach, but in a mixed discipline class it could lead to the complication of students not being familiar with the ideas or concepts being presented. It is also important that the audience is familiar with the papers the presentations are based on in order to be able to comment on how clearly the students have understood, explained and reacted to the content.

Project Introduction – Approaching a Topic

Over the course of *Academic Presenting and Presentations,* students are going to develop a presentation based on smart phones. This central topic was chosen as it is multi-disciplinary and could be approached from a wide range of academic fields.

Aim
To give students the opportunity to apply the learning of *Academic Presenting and Presentations* to a presentation developed through their own field of study

---

During this project introduction, the main focus will be explaining the task to the students and starting to think of a focus for their presentations. The topic "brainstorming session" encourages students to approach a topic and consider it from different perspectives. One of the interesting things about this project presentation will be having students present on the same central topic (smartphones) but approach it from different viewpoints depending on their fields of interest or academic study. The introductory text is very heavily referenced to help inspire different ways of thinking about smartphones, serving as a launch pad for considering smartphones from different perspectives.

You could encourage your students to think of a question they want answered, since an academic presentation is often the answer to a question, e.g.

- Why are iPhones so popular?
- What do most people use their smartphone for?
- What are the dangers of using smartphones?
- How might smartphones develop in the future?

- What were the key stages in smartphone development?
- How have smartphones affected people's relationships?
- How does the design of smartphone stores affect the brand?

Remind them that academic presentations are based on sources so they need to start reading to determine what they will present. The references of the input text could serve as a useful starting point. Emphasise to your students that the focus they choose now may change or evolve as they get more information. They could also conduct small research projects to collect evidence for their presentations.

Also remind them of the audience they are presenting to: their fellow students and you. As such their presentation has to be accessible and informative for that audience.

Project logistics

If you wish, you could change this from an individual presentation to a group presentation and adjust the presentation length to suit the logistics of your class.

There will be an opportunity for students to present their progress on their project after Unit 6, but prior to that make sure students are working on their projects. You could set aside a small amount of class time each week so they can outline their progress on their project. Putting students in a project study group may be a good idea so they can help each other along.

Unit 4
Elevator Pitch Poster Presentations

The elevator pitch is a style of presentation used in business to sell a concept quickly and efficiently. The general principles of an elevator pitch presentation can also be relevant to students in other disciplines as a way of focussing on the central message of their presentation and enabling them to present their ideas in a situation such as a trade fair or conference exhibition where they do not have long to engage the audience's attention.

Aims & Objectives
To raise students' awareness of the format and function of an elevator pitch poster presentation
- raise awareness of good design in visual aids
- provide strategies for dealing with group work and group presentations

---

While students may not be able to contribute much to the lead-in aims discussion about group work or elevator pitch presentations, based on the presentations they have seen so far as part of *Academic Presenting and Presentations*, they should have some ideas about what makes visual aids effective. Regarding the group work aspect, encourage students to consider if parts of a presentation should be separated so different members of the group work on different parts of the presentation or if there is another way to divide responsibilities.

Working in groups

Before looking at the genre of the elevator pitch presentation, the unit opens with a discussion on group work. This is because the group presentation is common in universities, either because of the learning benefits of working in teams or logistical concerns of dealing with a large cohort. This discussion should give you some valuable insight into your students' attitudes towards group work activities.

SP 4A – Managing Teamwork
This Sample Presentation has a dual function. It should give students some interesting information about teamwork and, in particular, highlight how different people can contribute to teams in different ways.

The task provided in the Student's Book involves looking at the visual aid used in the presentation and the post viewing discussion can cover areas like design, colour scheme, use of pictures and animation. Encourage students to suggest how the visual aids could have been improved and how effective the presenter's body language is.

Presentation Task 3

The purpose of this task is to get the students to cooperate in deciding their team name, flag and motto and also how to present to the rest of the group. Avoid giving any instruction to the effect that one particular person should present or telling them that all the members of the team should present. After the students have given their presentations, discuss the different approaches they took and, as a class, evaluate the advantages of the different approaches.

The follow-up reflective questions will also be useful for the students to consider how well the group work aspect of the activity went and help them recognise the role they currently naturally take in groups.

LP 4.1 – Group Presentations
The key learning point of this presentation is that every member of the group is responsible for the success of the presentation. An academic presentation is a coherent whole, with each part naturally leading to the next and building to a logical conclusion. As such, students should avoid compartmentalising the presentation into sections which they take individual responsibility for. A successful group presentation depends on the students developing a shared vision and agreeing the process of arguing towards their position.

Emphasise the importance of contingency planning: of having back-up presenters to the main presenter(s). The responsibility each member has to the team also has to be clear. It can be very off-putting in a group presentation if the members of the group do not pay attention to their colleagues when they are presenting or if they lose focus once their own contribution to the presentation is finished. Part of this responsibility also extends to every member of the group being able to answer questions on any aspect of the presentation.

Diplomatic language

Working in teams requires diplomacy and negotiation. Focus on some of the ways you can express disagreement in a positive and productive way.

Poster presentations

In an elevator pitch presentation, posters are a common form of visual aid. Posters are also a good starting point for getting students to think about visual aids in depth as the general principles of good poster design are transferable to more sophisticated presentation software visual aids. As well as the posters in the book, see if you can get access to posters that have been produced by the students in the institution you work in. It would be particularly motivating for your students to see what their peers have produced and what is expected of posters in their courses.

LP 4.2 – Designing A Poster
This Learning Presentation gives general advice about designing posters, considering readability, use of space etc. The main examples provided in the course of the presentation are of the kind of posters used in elevator pitch presentations where the emphasis is on impact.

You should also make your students aware that sometimes a poster may be designed for a different purpose. If the poster is going to form part of an exhibition, it has to be more informative and will contain more text.

Presentation Task 4

This task is for students to produce an elevator pitch presentation on a topic they have some ideas about, based on the discussions and inputs so far in this unit. Tell the students that the 30-second time limit means that their presentation has to be 30 seconds. Much shorter, or much longer (± 5 seconds), is unacceptable. One of the features of an academic presentation is that it is time bound and the students should be encouraged to practice good timing.

One of the things students may be tempted to do in an elevator pitch group presentation is some kind of choral statement/motto at the end of their pitch. This can be an effective tool (one main presenter and then everyone joining in to emphasise the final point) but if students go down this path make sure that they deliver the final message in unison.

Language focus

As outlined at the start of these notes, a central contention of *Academic Presenting and Presentations* is that full scripting of a presentation should be avoided. However, in the context of a 30-second pitch it is more important that the presentation have a strong clear message that is delivered within the required time. As such, scripting may be an advantage, but make sure when students are delivering their pitch presentations, they are not using a script or notes to do so.

This section also provides some advice on using notecards, which can be a valuable tool to help a presenter manage the presentation task. It would be good to have some card cut to an appropriate size so students can see what a notecard might look like. You could also ask them to revisit SP 4A and make notecards for the presentation. This would be a good opportunity to see how selective they are with the information they write on notecards and how useful their notecards would be.

Regarding scripting and notes you can emphasise a point raised in a couple of the LPs: that visual aids can serve as the notes for the presenter as long as they don't spend all their time reading the screen.

Presentation Task 5

This presentation task brings together the different things discussed over the course of Unit 4. If your students do not have access to printing facilities which can produce A1 posters, A3 would be acceptable for the purpose of seeing how they design a poster. Alternatively, the poster could be designed as a PPT slide which students show.

Encourage students towards creativity and variety of approach to this task. The presentation could begin with the description of an event, or a list of great leaders, or a list of attributes necessary for leadership.

You could introduce an element of competition here and have the class vote on which they think (apart from their own) was the most successful presentation and why. Returning to the lesson aim questions would also be useful during the planning and preparation phase of this task.

Unit 5
Persuasive Presentations

Academic presentations are commonly the articulation of an argument towards a particular point. This means that persuasion is a feature of academic presentations, but it is important to recognise that persuasion in an academic presentation does not depend on gimmicks, but on strength of academic argument.

Aims & Objectives
To focus students on the audience and provide them with strategies for encouraging the audience to accept their arguments
- provide strategies for opening a presentation
- consider elements that make an academic argument

You could extend the lead-in aims discussion to think about persuasion and the different ways we can be persuaded. Advertising might be a good topic to discuss. This will also serve as a good introduction to SP 5A, which is a presentation the students previously watched in Unit 2.

SP 5A
This is a persuasive presentation, perhaps a presentation by a lobbyist. When discussing the video, focus on the persuasive elements of the presentation e.g. personalisation, use of stress etc. and cross reference with the persuasive techniques outlined in this section. For the time being, do not draw attention to the fact that these persuasive techniques may not be appropriate in an academic presentation. The intention of the start of this unit is to familiarise students with the concept of persuasion and ways it could be achieved, before looking at the specifics of academic persuasion.

Presentation Task 6

This is quite a superficial task in the sense that it is not expected that the students research and collect support for their arguments. It will be a purely opinion-driven presentation to give students experience of delivering a persuasive presentation. This will also give them a presentation that they can reconsider when thinking about what makes for a successful *academic* persuasive presentation.

Topics are not limited to the three suggested in the book; this could be an opportunity to localise the material and bring in a topic relevant to your students. Rather than letting students decide their position, you could give them positions to take, one pair presenting in favour of the topic, one pair presenting against the topic and the rest of the class determining which presentation was more persuasive. Avoid letting the class turn into a debate, but during the preparation phase ask students to consider the alternative viewpoint and how they could deal with the opposing view in the course of their presentation. This idea of argument and counter argument is an important feature of academic presentations.

Research methods

In Unit 3 the concept of research was introduced. This unit builds on that by considering different types of research methodology. It is not expected that this will make students expert researchers, but rather make them aware of some of the issues involved in selecting a research methodology. Even if the only research they do is in class (be that interviews with fellow students or class surveys), it is important that they are aware of different ways of doing research and associated pros and cons of different methodologies. Read the text reproduced in this unit and discuss different research approaches. Students can draw on their own experience to help understand different research methods.

SP 5B – Choosing A Research Method
Before watching this Sample Presentation, go back to the discussion the group had on what made SP 5A persuasive and now draw their attention to the inappropriateness of some of the persuasive strategies e.g. personalisation. Ask students to reconsider what makes a presentation academic and suggest more appropriate techniques for making an academic presentation persuasive. Perhaps this could be developed into an evaluation sheet the students can use when watching the second Sample Presentation.

When students watch SP 5B, the main focus is on how persuasive they found it and how this persuasion was achieved. It could be valuable to watch the whole presentation the first time to determine if it is persuasive and then re-watch it, pausing at key moments to discuss how that persuasion is achieved e.g. the way the presenter introduces the topic, the use of referenced support, the clarity of the visuals aids, the use of animation to demonstrate mixing methodologies etc.

This is the first Sample Presentation which has a question and answer aspect. After the initial discussion on the presentation it would be worth going back and watching the Q&A part of the presentation again and evaluate how well the presenter dealt with the questions. Consider things like body language and how open the presenter seems to be to questions from the audience.

LP 5.1 – Being Persuasive In An Academic Presentation
By now the students should have a good idea what makes an academic presentation persuasive and it can be reinforced through this Learning Presentation. If the students developed an evaluation sheet in the previous activity this could be reviewed in light of the information in this presentation.

The key learning point of the presentation is that an academic presentation is persuasive in the same way an essay is persuasive: by the development of a logical argument supported by sources or evidence. Since this is a presentation course there is no need to go into great depth regarding the structure of argument, but emphasise the need for a clear progression in a presentation.

Presentation Task 7

So far in this course, support for presentations was either given to students (Unit 3) or not required (Unit 4). However, for this presentation students will need to find some support for their preferred methodology. They could be given some in-class research to do where they can use different methodologies and so base their opinion on experience. They could also generate their own support by doing in-class research into which research methodology people prefer. You could also offer some basic introductory texts that discuss strengths and weaknesses of research methods. Alternatively, it would also be a good opportunity to let the students conduct their own library or online research to come up with their own sources. There should be animated questions after each presentation.

The feedback for this presentation should revolve around how well argued and well supported it was. For the first time in the course, the academic integrity of the presentation matters.

Unit 6
Presenting Progress

During an extended project, students may be asked to give a progress presentation. This is an opportunity for people to see what they are doing and for them to get some valuable feedback on the direction they are taking.

Aims & Objectives
To enable students to present a project at an interim stage

- provide strategies for dealing with questions
- encourage students to consider use of PPT and other presentation software

Progress presentation outline

By now students should have a reasonable idea about how to structure a presentation. The first task in this unit, after the lead-in aims discussion, is a prediction of what the structure of a progress presentation should be. Get students to think of the structure as a series of steps they have to take, with each step moving the presentation forward.

The comparison of approaches suggested by students should highlight different approaches people took to the same task and, if the progression of the presentation is valid, this would be useful to demonstrate that structure is not 100% fixed and there is some leeway in how to approach a presentation as long as it successfully serves its purpose.

> **LP 6.1 – Presenting Progress**
> This Learning Presentation shows one of the possible variations by considering how the status of the project (if it is going well or badly) would impact the overall structure of the progress presentation. Comparison can be drawn with the structures the students proposed.

Language focus

Presenting progress is going to require students to talk about what they have done, what they are currently doing and what they still have to do. This will require using a full range of tenses and the exercise on page 81 of the Student's Book is an awareness-raising activity on appropriate tense usage. The exercise sentences are also useful indicators of the kinds of things students might be doing in the process of conducting an extended project. Depending on the language level of your students, you may or may not choose to discuss the use of perfect past and future tenses.

> **LP 6.2 – Using Presentation Software**
> In Unit 5 students considered how effectively visual aids were used in a persuasive presentation. This Learning Presentation focuses them on what makes for effective use of presentation software. The presenter focuses predominately on PowerPoint but it would be good to show students a Sample Presentation from alternative presentation software, like Prezi.
>
> The key learning point of the Learning Presentation is that presentation software is there to support a presentation, not dominate it.

Dealing with questions

The aspect of questions is a very important area of presenting. Throughout *Academic Presenting and Presentations* students should have been asking questions after the in-class peer presentations. They also saw a presenter dealing with questions in Unit 5. This should give them some ideas of strategies for dealing with questions.

When discussing the strategies, it should be stressed that a presenter should try to deal with the questions they are asked to the best of their ability.

- Panic and repetition are not positive strategies and should be avoided.
- Asking for clarification can gain valuable thinking time and may also make the focus of the question clearer.
- Reflection can be useful but should be done sparingly – the question was asked as the questioner wants to know what the presenter thinks.
- Deflection may be a reasonable response if the question is well off topic, but it can also suggest a lack of wider knowledge, so it better avoided.
- Admission is acceptable, although it can be avoided by preparing a presentation thoroughly.

SP 6A

This presentation is an opportunity to see a progress presentation in action, and also to see the presenter deal with difficult questions. One of the things to point out is that the questions arose because the presenter had a poorly designed project. It's important that a progress presentation gives the audience a clear idea of the project the presenter is working on. If something is going to be analysed, for example, what it is going to be analysed for, and how, has to be clear. You should emphasise that a progress presentation is an opportunity for the presenter to get feedback on how well designed their project is, and how it is going.

Project Review – Giving a Progress Presentation

Practice Presentation

Students should have been working on their smartphone presentations. This presentation will be a good opportunity to see what the focus of each presentation is and how well the students are progressing. At this stage they should have a clear focus or question that their final presentation is going to address and have done some of the background reading or research to begin to support their presentation (this research does not have to be especially robust or in-depth – class surveys or small scale interviews are fine).

It is also important for students to demonstrate a clear path and a realistic timeline of what they have left to do.

If their presentation is designed to answer a question, that question doesn't have to be fully answered in this presentation. Make sure the students are preparing a progress presentation explaining their project and where they are in it rather than a final presentation explaining their findings.

Unit 7
Problem/Solution Presentations

The problem/solution presentation has quite a lot of flexibility in terms of structure and shares a lot of similarities with recommendation presentations.

Aims & Objectives

To raise students' awareness of the different approaches to a problem/solution presentation

- raise students' awareness of plagiarism and how to avoid it
- raise student awareness of referencing conventions
- encourage students to avoid scripting a presentation

What is plagiarism?

This text introduces students to the concept of plagiarism and gives some examples of what plagiarism may involve. The two texts reproduced in this unit are good illustrations of plagiarism and effective paraphrase. You could ask your students to develop an effective paraphrase for the last paragraph of the text to give them an opportunity to practice avoiding plagiarism.

SP 7A

This is a well organised and clearly delivered problem/solution presentation. When watching this presentation, pause the video at the end of the presentation before the audience questions. Ask the students if they think it was a good presentation. Then ask if it was an effective academic presentation.

The lack of sources and referencing should be clear to them and, if not, re-emphasise just how important the use of support is in a presentation. When watching the question and answer section of the presentation, note how the first question concerns the lack of support.

Citing and referencing

While citing is something students should cover in an academic writing course, it is important that they have some awareness of the conventions of referencing. If the Anglia link doesn't work, there are many other universities which host similar interactive referencing guides. Comparing the reference slides of SP 4A and SP 5A will be a good illustration of how referencing shouldn't and should be done. As a follow-up exercise you could get the students to reformat the reference list for SP 4A correctly.

LP 7.1 – Problem/Solution

Before watching this Learning Presentation get the students to analyse the structure of the Sample Presentation and ask them to consider any alternative ways the presentation could have been organised. Compare their ideas with the structures proposed in LP 7.1.

Presentation Task 9

To try to reinforce the concept of not scripting a presentation, the basis of this task is proposing solutions to the issue of scripted presentations. The four texts shown in this context should enable the students to either propose solutions to the causes or effects of scripting, or both. During feedback consider how well the students used and successfully paraphrased the information from the input sources. Alternatively, students could give a presentation on a problem of their choosing but their presentation would have to be supported so would require more research time.

Unit 8
Research Presentations

This is the final presentation genre covered in *Academic Presenting and Presentations*, bringing together many of the issues and skills mentioned earlier in the course.

Aims & Objectives

To highlight the steps students should take in a research presentation to place their work in a wider context

- analyse the structure of research presentations to determine what makes a research presentation successful
- provide language for talking about graphs and data

The unit opens with a reminder of what research is. Now would be a good time to ask students to discuss what research they are carrying out/have carried out for their extended smartphone presentation project.

SP 8A

This is a good model presentation, which is well organised and effectively describes the research project and findings to the audience. However, in the discussion following the video, particularly in light of the questions the audience ask, consider as a class if something else could have been added to the presentation to make it more effective. Emphasise the need to anticipate things the audience may not understand and address this in the body of the presentation, time permitting.

Language Focus

Describing data will be an important part of student presentations. The language areas highlighted are the language of statistics and also the language of change and trends. The data provided in this section would give your students the opportunity to practice both of these. With the first data describing sales, make sure students don't try to describe the data in detail. A good exercise would be to increasingly limit the time they have to talk about the graph (30 seconds – 20 seconds – 10 seconds) to force them to be selective and determine what the key point they want to take from the graph is.

You could also take this opportunity to get students to practice presenting any data they may have gathered as part of their project.

LP 8.2 – Research Presentations
Before watching this Learning Presentation, get students to identify the steps the presenter took in SP 8A. Once they have a preliminary idea of structure, play the Learning Presentation and discuss as a group why each step has to be taken.

Project Presentation – Giving a Final Presentation

Congratulations. Your students are now at the end of *Academic Presenting and Presentations*. As the final capstone presentation, they should deliver their smartphone presentations. The A POINT planning sheet is provided to remind them to think about the features that make a presentation effective, with the additional criteria of support added to ensure they think about the academic aspect of the presentation.

Of all the presentations so far, this should be the most formal in terms of presenter dress, audience questions and expectations of quality. It is not required that the students have completed any primary research for this presentation, but they should certainly be drawing on sources they have read to develop their argument.

Rather than giving the audience any worksheets to complete as the presentation is being delivered, the evaluation of this presentation should be holistic – how effectively does the presenter engage the audience and deliver a clear support argument in their presentation?

Worksheets

The worksheets in the Student's Book can be used with any presentation given during this course or with any academic presentation given outside the context of the course. Some of the worksheets are designed to be used during the preparation stage; others are intended for use by the audience as a means of giving peer-group feedback on a presentation. There is some overlap in the coverage of the sheets so that participants can consider various aspects from slightly different perspectives.

They can also serve as inspiration for independently developed feedback and evaluation forms.

There is no set schedule for the use of these sheets as different students may benefit from different types of feedback at various phases of presenting and practising or might want to focus on different aspects of presenting at different times.

It is important to remember that a successful presentation is a presentation where all the different aspects of presenting reinforce each other.

Rationale

Introduction

Oral Presentations are an important part of studying in an English-medium university environment and will be something many students face, whatever their field of study. Such presentations can be particularly challenging for non-native English speakers (NNES) and consequently they will need support to develop their academic presentation skills. This rationale outlines the theoretical background and development of *Academic Presenting and Presentations*, a training course designed to help students cultivate academic presentation skills and deals with the various presentation tasks they may have to do as part of their university studies. A central tenet of the course is that effective presentation skills alone will not lead to a successful academic presentation. As well as technical presentation skills, students will also have to appreciate the key features of academic presentations (e.g. soundness of argument or use of referenced support) and also be aware of the expectations of different genres of academic presentation, from seminar presentations introducing a paper to more sophisticated research presentations. As such, each unit of *Academic Presenting and Presentations* focuses on a different presentation genre, building students awareness of not only how to present effectively, but how to present appropriately in an academic environment.

Why presentations?

Oral presentations are an important part of the undergraduate university experience (Alexander et al., 2008: p. 245). The Academic Support Clinic (ASC) of the Centre for English Language Education (CELE) in the University of Nottingham Ningbo China (UNNC) provides ongoing, in-session language and academic skill support for students throughout their degree-level studies. Over the course of the academic year 2011-12, there was opportunity to observe students delivering presentations for their lecturers and it was while watching Environmental Science research presentations that the particular challenges of an academic presentation became clear.

One of the first students approached the presentation in a time-honoured manner, outlining the topic and content in the introduction, presenting the information in the main body of the presentation, and summarizing the main points in the conclusion. The student had strong presentation skills, spoke confidently and clearly and, from an EAP tutor perspective, seemed to have dealt with the task well. When it came to question time, however, the substance of the presentation was seriously challenged by the student's lecturers, who highlighted the academic rigor expected from student presentations.

A later student, while not as linguistically competent or confident as the first, gave a presentation which was much more positively received by the lecturers. The student achieved this by approaching the structure of the presentation in a more sophisticated way. The presentation opened with a review of the current research and knowledge in the area, which led to identifying the gap in knowledge and outlining what the research project was designed to find out. The speaker then moved through the methodology of the chosen approach, presented the results and in the discussion and conclusion, returned to the research question and evaluated how successfully the research goal had been achieved. By transposing the structure of a written research assignment to an oral presentation, the student was able to deal with the assignment successfully and when it was time for questions from lecturers, the student was able to deal with the questions confidently and appropriately. Despite being at a linguistic disadvantage compared to the earlier presenter, this student was able to present *academically* more effectively by focusing on the purpose of the presentation and ensuring the audience was clear about the logical progression of the research project.

This observation is in line with a point made by Alexander et al. (2008: 249), that presentation feedback to students in an EAP context should focus on higher level task achievement (clarity of purpose, use of evidence) rather than surface language issues. This would suggest students have to be aware of the purpose of different types of presentation, and key features which make a presentation academic, in order to deliver an academic presentation successfully. The challenge students face is emphasized by a quick review of the various kinds of presentation students have to do during the first year of their degree programmes in the UNNC. In addition to the Environmental Science research presentations, presentation tasks range from informal seminar presentations of a paper the students have read to thirty-second poster pitch group presentations during which students have to try to sell an innovation. Architecture students have to manage maps, concept panels and models as they present their design to a close-questioning audience while Business students might be expected to give extended problem/solution presentations revolving around a company case study. This variety is not unique to UNNC: Zappa-Hollman (2007) investigates the differing expectations of presentations in History, Anthropology, Biochemistry and Neuroscience in a major Canadian university. Presentations are used as both formative and summative assessment tools, as well as a developmental process in and of themselves. Ultimately it may be a presentation task, a viva, which is the culmination of a student's academic career. In the way that NNES students may require additional support to develop an academic writing style it would also seem clear that they may require targeted support for developing their academic presentation skills as well (Alexander et al., 2008).

The UNNC context
UNNC is an English-medium university offering identical degree programmes to those of University of Nottingham UK. The student body is predominately

Chinese, with a small percentage (less than 10%) of non-Chinese students. These international students may be UK students on a campus exchange programme or students from countries as varied as Russia, Nigeria and Brazil following their full degree programmes at UNNC. To help students adjust to the expectations of 'Western' university education UNNC requires NNES students to do a foundation year, called the Preliminary Year, which is delivered by CELE and which focuses on developing student academic and language skills. Once students pass the Preliminary Year and enter their degree level studies, ongoing support is offered through the ASC.

One of the avenues of support open to students through the ASC is an academic advising service, whereby students can meet with an academic advisor to discuss an assignment they are working on or get help with a study-related issue they may be struggling with. Through watching a range of student draft presentations from students across different years of the university, it became apparent that the presentation workshops ASC offered to students, while superficially useful for developing generic presentation skills, were lacking in helping students deal with the full range of academic presentation tasks they may be faced with. Most of the feedback given to students by the ASC academic advisors was related to the organization and structure of student presentations rather than language-related issues. This may seem at odds with Alexander's contention that it could be delivery issues that students struggle with most in presentations (2008: 145), but in the same way that a student might have linguistically sophisticated writing skills (in terms of grammatical control and lexical flexibility) yet still find it difficult to write an academically sound essay, so might a student have effective presentation skills (in terms of delivery) and yet fail to deliver an academically sound presentation. That is not to say delivery issues are not important but to emphasise that students need to know what the expectations of an academic presentation are in order to present effectively and appropriately. They need to know what features make a presentation academic and develop strategies for dealing with and structuring different genres of presentation. The success of a presentation, from a subject lecturer viewpoint, seems to be on the delivery of a well argued, supported, logical presentation which demonstrates understanding of the topic rather than students simply demonstrating good presentation skills (Bolster, 2012). Hence the motivation to develop *Academic Presenting and Presentations*, a course designed to help prepare students to deliver university context presentations.

Current EAP oral presentation materials

When it comes to presenting in general, there are a number of training materials for oral presentations aimed at non-native speakers, e.g. *Presentations in English* (published by Macmillan). Within the academic context there are titles like *EAP Now!* (published by Pearson) that integrate presentation skills into a wider EAP course or a small number of stand-alone presentation skills titles: *Passport to Academic Presentations, University Foundation Study: Presentations – Module 11* (both published by Garnet Education) and *Giving Academic Presentations* (published by University of Michigan Press). University websites from Washington to Newcastle to Canberra give advice about academic presentations. So is there really a need for yet more presentation training material?

Quite simply, yes. Although there are materials available which provide sound advice about giving presentations, it is much harder to find materials aimed at NNES which delve into different genres of presentation, or which go much further into the structure and organization of a presentation beyond introduction-body-conclusion. This relative lack of clarity in training materials on the expectations and features of academic presentations is highlighted if we consider the stand-alone EAP oral presentation titles indicated earlier. For example, *Passport to Academic Presentations* (2008) focuses on technical presentation skills and presentation language, but only really considers informative and persuasive presentations as genres of presentation. Similarly, citing and referencing is an area which could reasonably be expected to feature prominently in an EAP presentation course, as referencing is arguably one of the central traits that makes a presentation academic, and yet across the three stand-alone EAP presentation titles it is seldom discussed in any depth. Particularly, when we consider the wealth of material dedicated to the development of student academic writing (with five dedicated academic writing titles published in the summer of 2012 alone: *Effective Academic Writing* series [OUP], *Progressive Skills* and *Reading & Writing 2012* [Garnet Publishing], *Four Point Reading & Writing Intro* [Michigan University Press] *Academic Writing Skills* [Cambridge]), the relative paucity of material aimed at academic oral presentations becomes clear.

Perhaps a contributing factor to the issues indicated in current EAP presentation materials is the fact that the area of academic oral presentations seems somewhat under-researched. It is difficult to find much discussion on what is expected of an academic presentation. Recognition of the challenges facing NNES when delivering academic presentations can be found in Zappa-Hollman (2007), which identifies different genres of presentation, gives a brief overview of steps taken in a presentation and also highlights the attributes which can contribute to a successful academic presentation. While Miles (n.d.) discusses academic presentations, reminding us that students taking a presentation course may have a motivation wider than learning presentation skills, the question of what makes a presentation academic is not addressed. Nor does Webster (2002) touch on this when outlining a Halliday-inspired genre approach to presentations. Formal speaking was clearly identified in Ferris' 1998 study as an area of concern amongst university students but, unfortunately, lacked insight as to which particular aspects of formal speech were of most concern. This indicates there isn't a wide body of research available for materials developers to drawn on.

Designing Academic Presenting and Presentations

These materials were developed in the context of UNNC. However, from the outset it was intended that the material be suitable for a more global audience and be suitable for use in a wide range of EAP contexts, by both developing presentation skills and touching on universal EAP themes like researching and plagiarism. An overview of course coverage can be seen in Appendix 1.

Which needs should be considered?

Targeting a potentially global audience automatically problematises the materials development process. As Graves (2000 p. 102) outlines, one of the foundations of course/materials development is a needs analysis and of the 10 aspects of needs she outlines, the first six of them relate to student needs. Within SLA theory there is also a strong call for focus on the needs of the learner (e.g. Hall's Need for Student-Centredness, 1995, cited in Tomlinson, 2007 p. 110) and the learner is also central when considering a proposal such as Krashen's comprehensible input i+1 principle (2003). If the needs of the learner are not central to materials design the validity and usefulness of the materials could be called into question.

Academic Presenting and Presentations was based on the observation of student needs in the ASC academic advising sessions, a service which was used by both Chinese and international students. As such there is an emphasis in the material on higher level task-achievement rather than discrete language points, since this seemed to be the area most students struggled with. It was determined however, for the purpose of this project, that an in-depth needs analysis of individual learners would be of limited benefit, given that the material is not being developed for a single class of students, but a much wider audience. It was also felt that, in this case, the needs of the context and other stakeholders were essential to the design of the scope and content of *Academic Presenting and Presentations*. What is more, by focusing on the context, some of the needs of the learners can be determined.

The intended students for *Academic Presenting and Presentations* will be young adults following a university education in an English-medium university, be this in an English-speaking country or an offshore university context such as UNNC.

Entrance to an English-medium university education usually requires an IELTS score or equivalent proof of English proficiency at the IELTS 5.5 level or above, indicating that the students are communicatively competent. They will typically be 18-22 years old, educated and their studying in an English-medium context would suggest they also have an international outlook. As discussed in Soureshjani and Ghanbari (2012), any presentation course will have to address areas of presenting which students feel are most important, helping students develop the details of their presentations, as well as helping with delivery issues such as body language and voice quality. Zappa-Hollman's (2007) findings that students need support with delivering presentations extemporaneously and managing the question and discussion stage of the presentation process were also influential in the design of *Academic Presenting and Presentations.*

Determining the needs of the student more closely is more difficult as their cultural background is unknown, as are their previous language learning experiences and preferred learning styles. However, what we know of language learning generally has also been considered in these materials. *Academic Presenting and Presentations* is highly authentic in terms of task and content type (Rubdy, in Tomlinson, 2007) and the students also get multiple exposure to teaching points which takes in to account Pienemann's teachability theory (Pienemann in Macaro, 2003) and Nunan's contention that learning does not follow predictable steps (Nunan in Carter & Nunan, 2004). Space has also been left for the local users (teachers) to adapt and supplement the materials to suit the needs of their local students. It is anticipated that material input will take one third of the teaching time, with another third being preparation time and the final third presentation time. As such there will be ample scope for teachers to address particular needs of students, e.g. specific pronunciation issues, or lexical development.

Graves (2000) points out that aside from the needs of the intended learners, it is also important to investigate the needs of other stakeholders, the context in which training will take place and the communicative skills students will need to develop. The importance of considering the needs of the context in ESP courses was later echoed by Barnard and Zemach (in Tomlinson, 2007). This being the case, rather than the needs being learner-focused *Academic Presenting and Presentations* is more directed to the needs of other stakeholders, the academic lecturers and the requirements of academic presentations. Regardless of student language ability the expectations of the presentations they have to perform are the same and, consequently, this course is designed with those expectations in mind.

Understanding the needs of academic presentations

With *Academic Presenting and Presentations* being geared towards the needs of the context, central to the success of the material was gaining an understanding of the expectations and requirements of presentations in the academic sphere. When preparing for this project, it was interesting to find how little has been written specifically about academic oral presentations. As Ferris and Tagg noted in 1996, not much work had been done exploring oral academic literacy. This lack of depth in the research field of academic presentations was later echoed by Miles (n.d.) although the issue is slowly being addressed. For example, Seliman and Naitim (unpublished) investigated the steps in English for Workspace presentations and Soureshjani and Ghanbari (2012) considered the factors which impact the effectiveness of an academic presentation. What is lacking, however, is any significant published research building on the findings of Zappa-Hollman (2007) describing the key features which contribute to a successful academic oral presentation (see Figs 1 and 2).

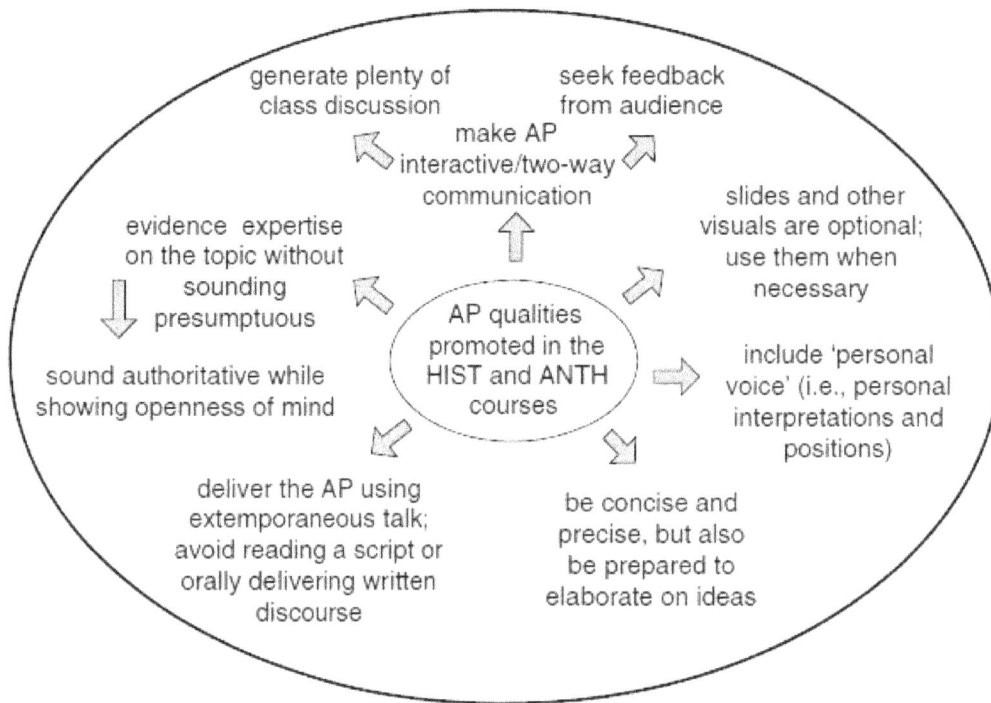

Fig 1: Positive Features of History or Anthropology Presentations (Zappa-Hollman, 2007)
AP = Academic Presentations, HIST = History, ANTH = Anthropology

Fig 2: Positive Features of Biochemistry or Neuroscience Presentations (Zappa-Hollman 2007)
AP = Academic Presentations, BIOC = Biochemistry, NRSC = Neuroscience

Fortunately, a project by Bolster (2012) further addresses this gap through a three-step process of interviewing academic lecturers, reviewing books for native English speakers designed to help develop academic presentations skills and conducting a criteria-driven evaluation of EAP presentation coursebooks. This resulted in a clear articulation of the requirements of an academic presentation and, consequently, of an EAP presentation course. The first step in the process of determining the needs of an academic presentation course was interviewing faculty staff. These interviews were video-recorded and covered issues of what kind of presentation tasks students had to do, the particular features which make a presentation academic and the factors which contributed to a successful presentation. The eight participating staff came from different academic disciplines: from Law and Architecture to Business and Environmental Science. There was also a mix of native and non-native speaker lecturers.

From the subject lecturer interviews the importance of the oral presentation in the university student experience was enforced and this held true across very different academic programmes. One of the main arguments in favour of the use of presentations seemed to be that a successful oral presentation requires students to truly understand a topic. The opportunity to question students directly on their work enables lecturers to see very quickly how deep a student's knowledge is. As one lecturer put it, a presentation is "the truest measure of mastery of the subject matter," (Bolster, 2012). A further argument in favour of using oral presentations is that presenting is a vital skill that students will need once they have completed their studies and so developing presentation skills also has a very practical aspect, a point which confirms the findings of Zappa-Hollman (2007). Interestingly, this was again a multidisciplinary perspective. The expectation was not just that business students would go on to do presentations at work, but that graduates from all the other faculties would also need to be able to present effectively in whatever future career they may follow.

Defining the scope of academic presentations

As outlined at the start of this paper, there are many types of presentation task which university students may be asked to do, from formal assessments to informal seminar presentations. The thing that unites them, however, is that they take place in the university sphere and it could be argued that there are common expectations that cut across different academic disciplines. The interviews in Bolster (2012) and Zappa-Hollman (2007) made clear the rigorous standards lecturers have when it comes to presentations and that they are viewed in a similar light to academic essays. Indeed, it seems that while the medium may differ (oral and written) the key features of academic discourse are similar, with a clear parallel in the expectations of a good written assignment and a successful oral presentation. Issues such as overall structure, logical progression and firmly rooted conclusions based on reliable and verifiable evidence are as much a factor in oral presentations as in essays (Bolster, 2012). Oral presentations are also very much seen as a communicative act and the ability to make complex arguments or issues accessible to a wider public is highly valued (Bolster, 2012). A particular challenge of an oral presentation, however, is that students are expected to be able to articulate a knowledge outside of the content of the presentation. Where an academic essay represents the student's complete answer, in an oral presentation the student's ideas and arguments are open to questioning and it was widely felt by the lecturers that the question and answer stage of the presentation was the most valuable and insightful (Bolster, 2012). Essentially, an academic oral presentation contributes to, or promotes, further discussion (Bolster, 2012, Zappa-Hollman, 2007).

The scope and coverage of *Academic Presenting and Presentations* is therefore based on the following understanding of academic presentations, drawing together experience of working in the ASC and ideas from the papers outlined previously.

- An oral academic presentation is a clear articulation of ideas, based on and referencing sources or research evidence, in which the presenter leads the audience to logical and sound conclusions. Effective presentation skills are needed so the audience can follow the presentation easily, but an academic presentation must have substance. Through the presentation the presenter must analyse and evaluate information, making their reaction and position clear to the audience. Information in an academic presentation must be verifiable and the presenter must have a wider and deeper knowledge of the topic than that presented in the body of the presentation. A presentation should lead to discussion and further debate, with the presenter able to respond to audience questions competently. Different genres of academic presentation (e.g. presenting a paper, research presentations or problem-solution presentations) will require students to employ an appropriate structure.

General principles of material design

When developing any training material, a wide range of choices need to be made at the outset, from the course coverage and medium to methodology. *Academic Presenting and Presentations* was designed taking into account Evans and Morrison's (2010) contention that EAP materials need to help develop learner's language and skills. The practical nature of a presentation course means that the material must be highly skills focused, but also recognise the particular language issues non-native speakers may experience when giving presentations, e.g. pronunciation concerns or questions about using appropriate lexis, both in the content of the presentation and the language of presenting itself. The material uses a lot of video inputs and could potentially exist in a self-access virtual environment but the very nature of presenting requires a group dynamic so presentations can be practiced in front of an audience. This resulted in a course-book based set of materials. A presentation course also requires a greater focus on oral than written production although, as the course developed, the very nature of academic presentations meant that other skills are touched on.

One of the main aims in designing the material was to avoid the criticism levelled by Harwood of simply repeating what has previously been done (2005 p. 152). For this reason, no other presentation books were looked at until the overall design and functionality of the material had been established. This was based on the following overarching principles, developed through experience of student presentations and influenced by the literature outlined above.

- There is no 'right' way to present, so observing and analysing multiple sample presentations will enable students to identify positive (and negative) presentation features; the course contains eleven different sample presentations across different genres of academic presentation.
- Students need ample opportunities to present in order to overcome nerves or fear of presenting and develop their own presentation style; there are eleven main presentation tasks in *Academic Presenting and Presentations*.
- Students have to develop competency in delivering different genres of academic presentation; there are six genres of academic presentation covered in the course.
- A successful academic presentation is about more than demonstrating good presentation technique; the presentation must be academically sound (see Unit 2).
- All of the presentation tasks the students are asked to do should fully reflect the type of presentations they may face in their academic studies.
- Academic presentations are time-bound, so there can be low tolerance for over-complex signposting language or padding.
- An academic presentation should avoid overt presentation gimmicks but be engaging to motivate listening and later discussion (see Unit 5).
- Academic presentations must be supported by factual information; personal opinion alone is not adequate (see Unit 7).

When it comes to that overall design the intention was to develop materials that were theoretically sound and also practitioner friendly. The work of Tomlinson (in Tomlinson, 2007) outlining guiding principles for materials was invaluable and ensured the emphasis was on producing material which was accessible, interactive, engaging, and needs-driven, qualities also valued by Dat (in Tomlinson, 2007) when discussing the materials designed for the development of speaking skills.

Course methodology

The importance of the methodology of materials cannot be overstated, especially as we are arguably in a time of "text-book defined practice" (Akbari, 2008 p. 647).

While no single teaching methodology dominates these materials, their development and design were very much influenced and informed by three main threads, although only aspects of each were incorporated into the course design.

Observe-Hypothesise-Experiment (Lewis, 1993)

The Observe-Hypothesise-Experiment (OHE) cycle was proposed within the Lexical Approach, but its application in *Academic Presenting and Presentations* is in the observation of presentations, hypothesising about what makes an academic presentation successful and experimenting through preparing and delivering a range of presentations. Although the Lexical Approach as a whole has faced criticism, notably in Thornbury (1998), this has been centred more on the validity of placing language chunks at the centre of language learning rather than on the OHE cycle itself. Rather than focusing on building awareness of collocations the OHE cycle in *Academic Presenting and Presentations* is used to raise awareness of presentation features, be they linguistic, structural or related to delivery. Throughout the course, students will be expected to notice, to watch video presentations and consider issues like organisation and language. In this way, they can build a profile of what they think works in a presentation and use it to develop their own presentation style. There are many different ways to present successfully, so rather than telling students what makes a successful presentation and trying to get them to present in that way, it is more beneficial to put a wide range of options in front of them and let them choose what works for them personally.

Genre analysis (Hyland, 2007)

In the way students may be expected to use certain steps during different types of essay, they should use similar steps in different types of presentation, as indicated in Seliman & Naitim (2010) and Zappa-Hollman (2007). For this reason, *Academic Presenting and Presentations* is not arranged thematically or around a particular presentation skill, but rather by presentation genre, starting with the most accessible (Unit 3 - presenting a paper) and ending with arguably the most complex (Unit 8 - presenting a (research) project). In this way, each genre can be considered and its key features and steps highlighted - how a persuasive presentation may begin is very different to how a research presentation should begin, for example (see Units 5 and 8). This means going deeper into the structure of a presentation than simply introduction-body-conclusion, although the course avoids the temptation of being overly prescriptive. Within a single presentation there may be problem/solution, informative and persuasive elements so students will be encouraged to structure their presentations based on the objective of their presentation and the audience. For instance, when presenting a paper in a seminar, there are expectations of things students should do (e.g. adding a layer of evaluation and interpretation over simple reporting) that need to be highlighted to ensure successful completion of the task.

Content-based instruction (Richards & Rogers, 2006)

Topic selection for *Academic Presenting and Presentations* was carefully considered and although the course does not adopt a full Content and Language Integrated Learning (CLIL) approach as outlined in Coyle, Hood & Marsh (2010) in terms of being completely content-driven and aiming to encourage cognitive flexibility, it does borrow from the idea that content should be relevant and beneficial to learners in its own right, regardless of its later exploitation for language or presentation skill development. The initial plan was to have material that revolved around renewable energies, as this is both topical and potentially multi-disciplinary. However, as the course developed it was recognised that an extra layer of benefit could be added by changing the topic focus. Rather than, for example, students looking at a problem/solution presentation about new energy sources for a city, more could perhaps be gained by changing the topic to the problem/solution of plagiarism in academic work (see Unit 7). This approach would mean both students' presenting skills and wider academic skills and knowledge could be developed simultaneously. As an illustration of how this works in practice, in the unit on presenting a paper (Unit 3) the papers students have to read and present are introductory texts to research. This initial discussion on the nature and purpose or research serves as a launch pad for the research project students will undertake later in the course. Additionally, the use of video presentations as the main input tool for the course also gives students extra opportunities to identify successful presentation techniques.

Academic Presenting and Presentations

The starting principle of *Academic Presenting and Presentations* was that presenting is a skill that can only be developed through practice and that exposure to a range of examples would enable students to identify aspects of presenting they could use themselves. Rather than the somewhat clichéd approach of showing students a staged negative example (a poor presenter who speaks in a monotone, fumbles notes etc.) and a polished positive example, it was decided that only authentic presentations be used during the course, each with relative strengths and weaknesses. No presentation in the course is without fault, but there should always be some positive features that students could potentially incorporate into their own presentation repertoire. Similarly, students will be encouraged when watching peer presentations to identify both positive features and areas which could be improved, both for the benefit of the presenting student, and the peer observer.

A presentation-driven course

During *Academic Presenting and Presentations* students watch a lot of video presentations and while this may lack variety and lean more towards the preference of visual learners, the benefit of exposing students to different types of presentation and presenting cannot be discounted. To ensure fully authentic delivery, none of the presentations were scripted in advance, thus enhancing the opportunity to demonstrate authentic language items and presentation techniques. There are two different types of presentation used in the course, Sample Presentations and Learning Presentations.

The eleven Sample Presentations illustrate various types of presentation to the students and the emphasis while watching these presentations will be on seeing how different presentations work and how a presentation can be delivered successfully.

The sixteen Learning Presentations take on more of a teaching role, giving students information and advice about different aspects of presenting.

Course components

The main components of *Academic Presenting and Presentations* are the Student's Book, the accompanying video material (Sample Presentations and Learning Presentations), the worksheets included at the back of the Student's Book and this Teacher's Book. The Student's Book is arranged linearly, with the expectation that students progress through the units in sequence. The material in the Student's Book is supplemented by additional/alternative activities set out in this Teacher's Book. This enables the class teacher to vary and expand the focus of the course according to student needs.

A Flexible Course

Academic Presenting and Presentations is designed for flexible delivery. Students will be given a directing focus when watching presentations in the Student's Book but the worksheets in the Student's Book can also be used to encourage students to focus on particular aspects of the presentations, e.g. academic integrity, structure, delivery or body language etc. These sheets can be used both with the presentations provided in the course and to guide peer feedback of in-class student presentations. This allows the classroom teacher to direct activities towards the needs of their students and could result in different students watching the same presentation and yet looking at different features.

As well as the presentations students have to produce throughout the course, there is also an extended project which leads to the students' final presentation. This project is an opportunity for students to apply the learning from *Academic*

Presenting and Presentations to their own field of study. Although the central topic for all students will be the same – smartphones – they will be able to approach the topic from their own discipline so they could look at marketing aspects, the impact on personal communications, health effects or design features, depending on their degree programme. Giving students the scope to decide the focus of their presentation and observing how students from different disciplines approach the same central topic should keep the project motivating.

Academic Presenting and Presentations raises learner awareness of different genres of academic presentation and highlights the key features that make a presentation academic. Students get a great deal of exposure to academic presentations and many opportunities to produce academic presentations of their own. Useful presentation language is highlighted as are other language related aspects of presentations, such as use of voice. Students who complete the course are not going to be perfect presenters, but they should be students who understand the expectations of an academic presentation and present accordingly.

Criteria-driven evaluation of *Academic Presenting and Presentations*

As part of the Bolster (2012) project, criteria were developed to evaluate published EAP academic presentation materials. These criteria were applied to *Academic Presenting and Presentations* by the same three evaluators who had evaluated the published training materials as part of the Bolster project, following the same procedures. *Academic Presenting and Presentations* was reviewed very positively, scoring highly on both the overall impressionistic score (an average of 87% positive) and the more objective criteria-based evaluation (an average of 82% positive), leading to an overall score of 83% (see Appendix 2 for full results). This compares favourably to the evaluation of the three published academic presentation coursebooks (see Tables 1 & 2 below, data taken from Bolster, 2012).

Comparison of Material Evaluation Results: Overview

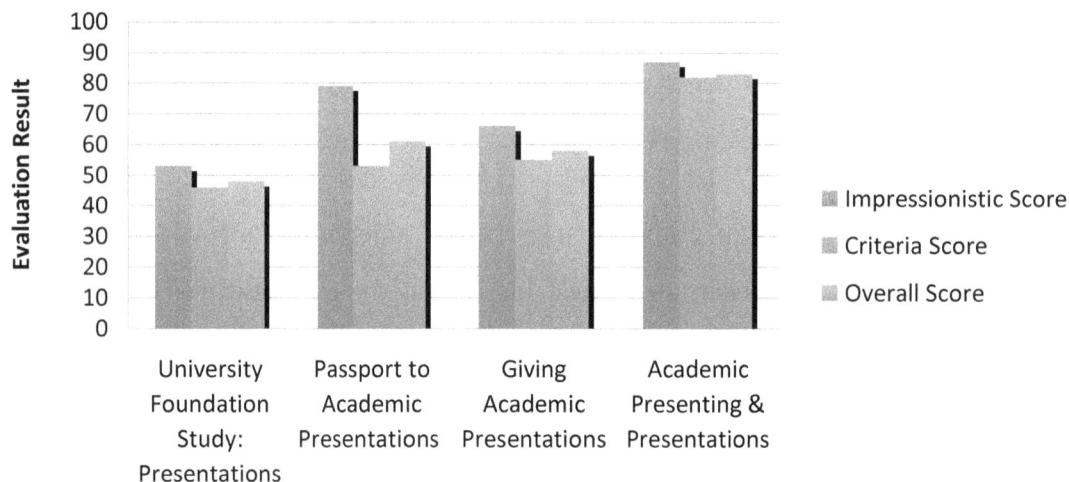

Table 1: *Overview of Evaluation Results*

Comparison of Material Evaluation Results: By Criteria Categories

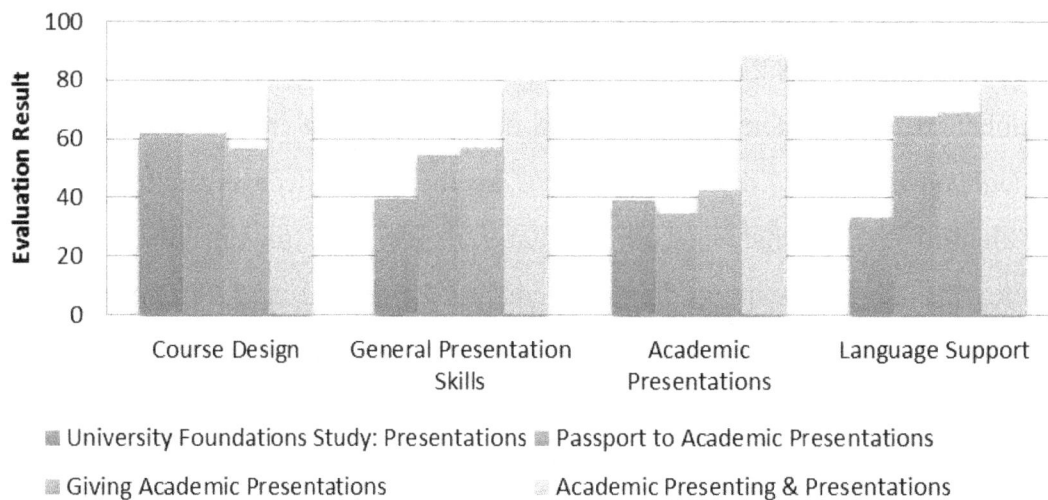

Table 2: *Comparison of Evaluation Results by Criteria Category*

It is particularly encouraging that *Academic Presenting and Presentations* scored highly on the Academic Presentation criteria, suggesting the course should be successful in helping students understand the expectations of academic presentation tasks.

Conclusions

Oral academic presentations are an important aspect of the university student experience and an area which could be more fully researched. Similarly, more could be done to develop targeted training materials to help NNES deal with academic presentation tasks successfully. *Academic Presenting and Presentations* is designed to serve as a useful resource for NNES students. By tackling separate academic presentation genres and focussing students' attention on the key features of oral academic presentations, it is hoped the course will enable students to both present well and, more pertinently, present well academically.

Bibliography

Akbari, R (2008) Postmethod Discourse and Practice. *TESOL Quarterly* Volume 42, Issue 4, pp. 641-652

Alexander, O, Argent, S & Spencer, J (2008) *EAP Essentials: A Teacher's Guide To Principles & Practice.* Reading: Garnet Publishing Ltd.

Barnard, R & Zemach, D (2007) Materials for Specific Purposes. In B. Tomlinson, ed. *Developing Materials for Language Teaching.* London: Continuum

Bell, D (2008) Passport to Academic Presentations. Reading: Garnet Education.

Bolster, A (2012) Materials Evaluation Survey of EAP Presentation Materials. MA Dissertation. Leeds Metropolitan University

Coyle, D, Hood P and Marsh, D (2010) Content and Language Integrated Learning. Cambridge: Cambridge University Press.

Dat, B (2007) Materials For Developing Speaking Skills. In B. Tomlinson, ed. *Developing Materials for Language Teaching.* London: Continuum

Evans, S and Morrison B (2010) 'The first term a university: implications for EAP'. *ELT J* first published online November 25, 2010 doi:10.1093/elt/ccq072

Ferris, D (1998) Students' Views of Academic Aural/Oral Skills: A Comparative Needs Analysis. *TESOL Quarterly* Vol 32, Issue 2, pp. 289-316)

Ferris, D and Tagg, T (1996) Academic oral communication needs for EAP learners: what subject-matter instructors actually require. *TESOL Quarterly*, Vol. 30, pp. 31–58

Graves, K (2000) Designing Language Courses: A Guide for Teachers. Boston, MA: Heinle & Heinle

Harwood, N (2005) What do we want EAP materials for? *Journal of English for Academic Purposes* Volume 4, Issue 2, pp. 149-161

Hyland, K (2007) *English for Academic Purposes: An Advanced Resource Book.* Oxon: Routledge.

Krashen, S (2003) Explorations in Language Acquisition and Use. Portsmouth: Heinemann

Lewis, M (1993) *The Lexical Approach: The State of ELT and a Way Forward.* Hove: Language Teaching Publications

Macaro, E (2003) Teaching and Learning a Second Language – A Guide to Recent Research and its Application. New York: Continuum

Miles, R (n.d.) 'Oral Presentations for English Proficiency Purposes'. *Reflections on English Language Teaching*, Vol. 8, No. 2, pp. 103–110 [Online]. Available at: http://www.nus.edu.sg/celc/research/relt/files/Vol8_2/103-110miles.pdf [21/6/2012]

Nunan, D (2004) Second Language Acquisition. In R. Carter & D. Nunan, ed. *The Cambridge Guide to Teaching English to Speakers of Other Languages*. Cambridge: Cambridge University Press

Richards, J and Rodgers, T (2006) Approaches and Methods in Language Teaching. New York, Cambridge University Press

Rudby, R (2007) Selection of Materials. In B. Tomlinson, ed. *Developing Materials for Language Teaching*. London: Continuum

Seliman, S & Naitim, M (2010) The Genre Of The Body Of Oral Presentations Delivered By English For Workplace Communication Students, pp. 1-9. (Unpublished). Available at http://eprints.utm.my/10452/ (accessed 9 September 2012)

Soureshjani, K & Ghanbari, H (2012) Factors Leading to An Effective Oral Presentation in EFL Classrooms. *The TFLTA Journal (online)*, Vol 3, pp. 37-50. Available at: http://www.tflta.org/uploads/1/0/6/9/10696220/tfltajournal3.pdf#page=37 (accessed 9 September 2012)

Thornbury, S (1998) The Lexical Approach: A Journey Without Maps. *Modern English Teacher* Vol 4, Issue 7, pp. 7-13

Tomlinson, B (2007) Developing Principled Frameworks for Materials Development. In B. Tomlinson, ed. *Developing Materials for Language Teaching*. London: Continuum

Webster, F (2002) A Genre Approach To Oral Presentations. *The Internet TESL Journal*. Available at http://iteslj.org/Techniques/Webster-OralPresentations.html (accessed 9 September 2012)

Zappa-Hollman, S (2007) Academic Presentations across Post-secondary Contexts: The Discourse Socialization of Non-native English Speaker. *The Canadian Modern Language Review*. Vol 63, N. 4, pp.455-485

www.ingramcontent.com/pod-product-compliance
Lightning Source LLC
Chambersburg PA
CBHW080522090426
42734CB00015B/3134